Butterfly Fun

Activity Book

Jessica Mazurkiewicz

Dover Publications, Inc.
Mineola, New York

Bibliographical Note

Butterfly Fun Activity Book is a new work, first published by
Dover Publications, Inc., in 2009.

International Standard Book Number

ISBN-13: 978-0-486-47198-3
ISBN-10: 0-486-47198-5

Manufactured in the United States by Courier Corporation
47198503
www.doverpublications.com

Note

This little book is full of fun activities featuring one of your garden's prettiest creatures—the butterfly! Here you will learn interesting butterfly facts as you complete mazes, word searches, codes, follow-the-dots, crossword puzzles, as well as counting and matching games. You can even learn to draw your very own butterfly! Try your best to complete each activity, but if you get stuck, you can turn to the solutions section, which begins on page 53. When you finish the activities, you can have even more butterfly fun by coloring in the pages with crayons, colored pencils, or markers. Let's fly!

Connect the dots to see this butterfly's favorite perch.

Here are eight butterfly friends. Find and circle the one with the most spots.

Bella Butterfly is relaxing in her garden.

This picture of Bella looks the same as the one on the previous page, but it's not. Find and circle six things that are different.

Unscramble the letters to learn one place where a butterfly gets its food.

How many butterflies can you count? Write the number in the square on the tree stump.

This little butterfly is lost! Can you help him find his friends at the end of the path?

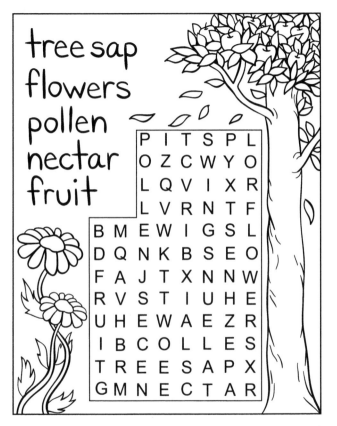

tree sap
flowers
pollen
nectar
fruit

P	I	T	S	P	L
O	Z	C	W	Y	O
L	Q	V	I	X	R
L	V	R	N	T	F
B	M	E	W	I	G	S	L
D	Q	N	K	B	S	E	O
F	A	J	T	X	N	N	W
R	V	S	T	I	U	H	E
U	H	E	W	A	E	Z	R
I	B	C	O	L	L	E	S
T	R	E	E	S	A	P	X
G	M	N	E	C	T	A	R

Some things that butterflies eat are listed above. Find and circle them in the puzzle. Look down and across.

11

The five caterpillars shown above are hiding in the garden on the next page.

Find and circle the five hidden caterpillars.

D=1 M=2 I=3 A=4 G=5 W=6

Every year we

2	3	5	7	4	8	10

to a warm
place
for the
Winter.

Manny the Monarch has some special messages for you
on this page and the one opposite.

R=7　T=8　K=9　E=10　L=11

Our favorite
food is

2	3	11	9	6	10	10	1

Use the number code to figure out the messages. Write the letters in the boxes. Then read what Manny has to say!

These butterflies are happy in a garden of daisies!

Find and circle the six things that make this picture different from the one on the left.

All these butterflies look very similar, but only two
are identical. Draw a line between the two that are the
same.

18

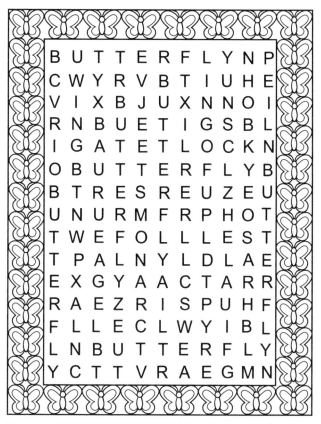

```
B U T T E R F L Y N P
C W Y R V B T I U H E
V I X B J U X N N O I
R N B U E T I G S B L
I G A T E T L O C K N
O B U T T E R F L Y B
B T R E S R E U Z E U
U N U R M F R P H O T
T W E F O L L L E S T
T P A L N Y L D L A E
E X G Y A A C T A R R
R A E Z R I S P U H F
F L L E C L W Y I B L
L N B U T T E R F L Y
Y C T T V R A E G M N
```

The word BUTTERFLY is hidden in the puzzle seven times. Search down and across to find and circle them all.

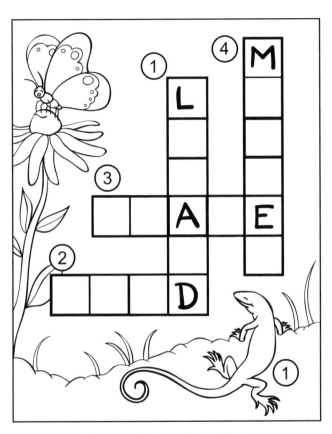

Some animals eat butterflies!

20

The number next to each animal tells you where it belongs in the puzzle.

Connect the dots to find out where this butterfly is about to land.

The letters B, U, T, T, E, R, F, L, and Y are hidden in the picture above. Find and circle them all.

Bobby Butterfly has something to tell you! Use the number code to write the words on the correct blanks. Then read the message.

24

Decorate this butterfly by drawing a pretty pattern on her wings.

Follow the lines from the butterfly and the caterpillar to see who will perch on the flower.

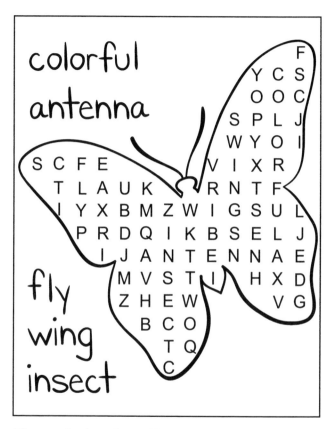

colorful

antenna

S C F E
T L A U K
I Y X B M Z W I G S U L
P R D Q I K B S E L J
I J A N T E N N A E
M V S T I H X D
Z H E W V G
B C O
T Q
C

F
Y C S
O O C
S P L J
W Y O I
V I X R
R N T F
F
U

fly

wing

insect

Five words about butterflies are listed above. Find and
circle them in the puzzle. Search down and across.

27

Butterflies love sunflowers!

This picture looks like the one on the previous page, but
there are six differences. Find and circle them all.

There are three pairs of matching butterflies. Draw a line
to connect each pair.

Connect the dots to help this caterpillar grow into a beautiful butterfly.

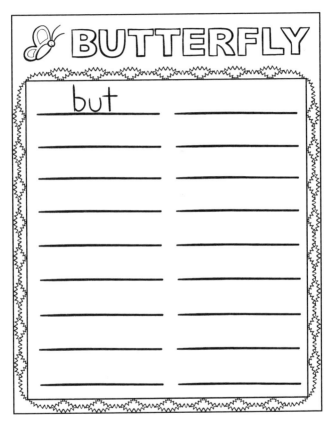

BUTTERFLY

but

See how many words you can make using the letters in BUTTERFLY. If you run out of room, write more words on a separate paper.

32

Four things in this picture don't belong. Find and circle them.

S=1 R=2 I=3 N=4 C=5

I hatched out of a

								|.
5	8	2	10	1	6	7	3	1

Use the number code to fill in the blanks on this page and the one opposite.

A=6 L=7 H=8 O=9 Y=10

My friend the moth hatches from a

5	9	5	9	9	4

Now you can find out what the butterfly is saying!

This animal tries to catch butterflies. Connect the dots to find out what it is.

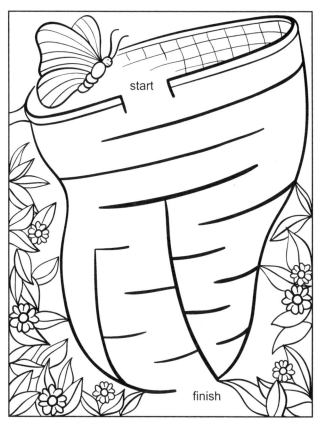

start

finish

Help this butterfly escape the dangerous net by guiding her through the maze.

Swallowtail　　　Painted lady

```
        J S X N N
      B M E W I G S B L
    W A P E A C O C K N U
    O C K J L X N N W J T
    Y T R V S L E U Z E S T
    B L U E M O R P H O E W
    T W E S O W L L E S C E
    A P A I N T E D L A D Y
    X G M A A C T A R T
        R I S P
        C L W Y
        H V I X
        V R N T
```

Blue Morpho

Peacock　　　　　　　Monarch

Find and circle the butterfly names in the puzzle above.
Look down and across.

Only one of these four butterflies can fit into the space in the leaf. Find and circle the butterfly that fits.

Look carefully at the happy butterflies on this page and
the one opposite.

40

Find and circle six things that make this picture different
from the other one.

A=1 E=2 I=3 O=4 U=5

d			s	y
	1	3		

g		l	d		n	r		d
	4			2			4	

s		n	f	l		w		r
5					4		2	

Butterflies feed on many different kinds of plants, as you
can see here and on the opposite page.

42

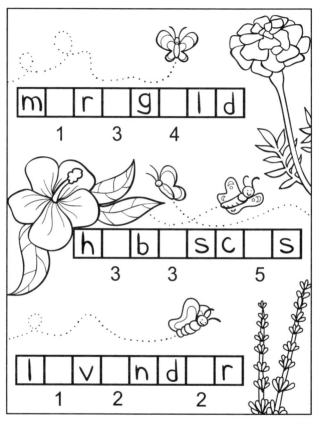

m		r		g		l	d
	1		3		4		

h		b		s	c		s
	3		3			5	

l		v		n	d		r
	1		2			2	

Use the number code to learn the plant names. Write each missing letter where it belongs in the puzzles.

These six butterflies all look the same, but one is different. Find and circle the one that is different.

You can learn to draw a butterfly by following the three simple steps shown above. Draw your pictures in the frame.

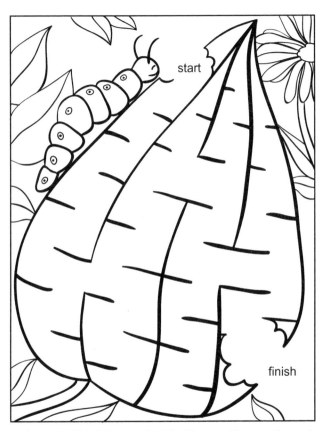

start

finish

This caterpillar is hungry! Help him eat his way through the leaf.

Unscramble the letters and write them in the blanks to spell a word telling where a butterfly finds food.

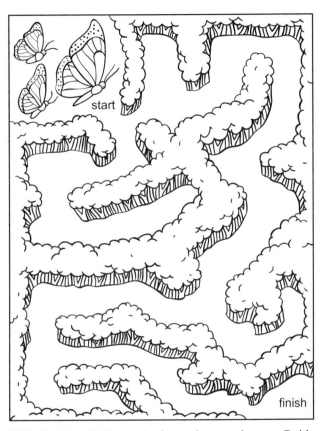

start

finish

This family of Monarchs is ready to migrate. Guide them through the maze of trees.

All butterflies have six legs. Count the legs on each butterfly, and then circle the butterflies that have the correct number of legs.

There are four things in this picture that don't belong.
Find and circle them.

☐ Dragonfly

☐ Ladybug

☐ Butterfly

[2] Caterpillar

Put these insects in alphabetical order by writing a number in the blank square next to its name. One is done for you.

This butterfly would like a snack. Guide it through the maze of leaves to the delicious flower.

SOLUTIONS

page 4

page 5

page 7

page 8

54

page 9

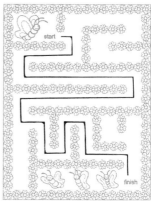

page 10

page 11

page 13

55

D=1 M=2 I=3 A=4 G=5 W=6

Every year we

M	I	G	R	A	T	E
2	3	5	7	4	8	10

to a warm
place
for the
Winter.

page 14

R=7 T=8 K=9 E=10 L=11

Our favorite
food is

M	I	L	K	W	E	E	D
2	3	11	9	6	10	10	1

page 15

page 17

page 18

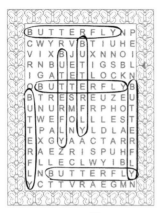

page 19

page 20

page 22

page 23

page 24

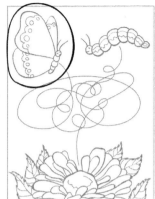

page 26

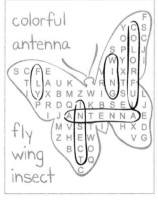

page 27

page 29

58

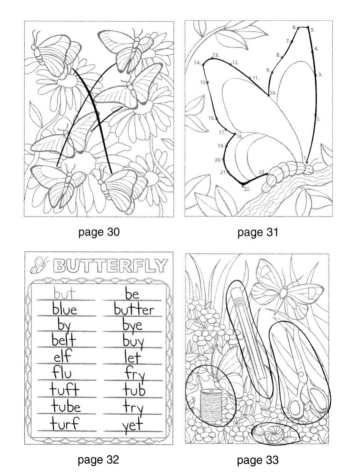

page 30

page 31

BUTTERFLY

but	be
blue	butter
by	bye
belt	buy
elf	let
flu	fry
tuft	tub
tube	try
turf	yet

page 32

page 33

S=1 R=2 I=3 N=4 C=5

I hatched out of a

c	h	r	y	s	a	l	i	s
5	8	2	10	1	6	7	3	1

page 34

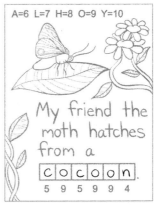

A=6 L=7 H=8 O=9 Y=10

My friend the moth hatches from a

c	o	c	o	o	n
5	9	5	9	9	4

page 35

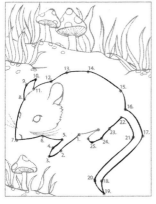

page 36

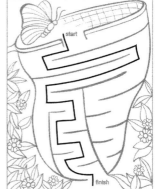

page 37

page 38

page 39

page 41

page 42

page 43

page 44

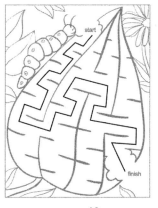

page 46

page 47

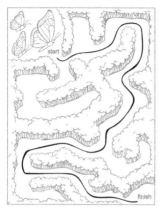

page 48

page 49

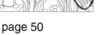

page 50

page 51

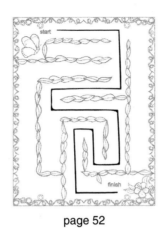

page 52